Easy New Orleans

For Beginners

Southern House Publishing

Copyright © 2020 Southern House Publishing

All rights reserved.
No part of this book may be reproduced in any form
by electronic, mechanical or other means
without prior permission from the publisher.

ISBN: 978-1-9997478-6-2

tylermusic.co.uk

CONTENTS

Introduction	1 - 2
Chord Progressions	3 - 6
Audio And Fingering	7 - 7
New Orleans Rhythms	8 - 9
New Orleans Bass Style 1	10 – 19
Broken Chord Runs	20 - 26
Broken Run Riffs	27 - 29
Mardi-Gras Type Groove	30 - 32
Split Chord Patterns	33 - 35
Set-Ups	36 - 40
Triplet Feel Blues	41 - 46
8-Bar Blues	47 - 50
Second-Line Groove	51 - 58
New Orleans Groove	59 - 64
Practice Suggestions	65 - 65
Suggested Listening	66 - 66
Downloadable Audio Access	67 - 67

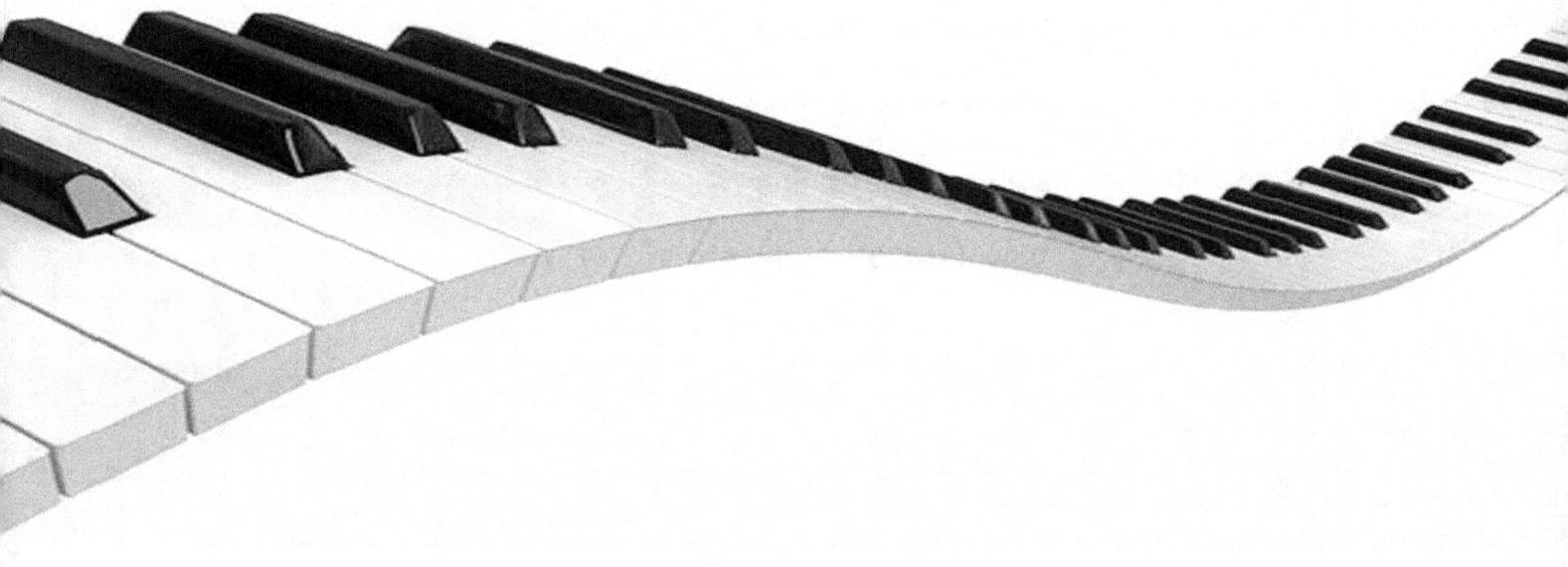

Introduction

If you are reading this, then I assume that you have an interest in the music of New Orleans, and in particular the blues that grew up in this area. And seeing as this is a tuition book, you obviously have an interest in playing this on the piano, so I will start by congratulating you on having great taste in both music and instruments.

New Orleans blues is a subgenre of blues music that is considered to have developed (or became popular) around the 1940s and 1950s in and around – as if you couldn't guess – the city of New Orleans. It is an interesting style of music, as although it is rooted in the blues, it is very much a style to itself, being heavily influenced by strong Caribbean rhythms. So although it may have a similar structure as other blues styles, it has its own unique feel.

The purpose of this book is to give those that are new to New Orleans piano a first step into the style. Its aim is to cover the basics and get you started, the examples begin easy and then gradually increase in difficulty while introducing a few extra elements along the way. Once you have the basics that this book provides, you'll be at a point to progress further with other publications of a higher difficulty level. And/or by using some of the sheet music that's available and hopefully from listening to the music too.

Thanks for reading this little intro, I hope you will find this book helpful on the start of your musical journey, and I further hope that you will continue on, helping to keep the music alive. But most of all, just enjoy it, it's what music was made for.

12-Bar Blues Progression

New Orleans blues piano can be seen to use various chord progressions, which includes the first one we will look at, the 12-bar blues progression.

The 12-bar blues progression in its most basic form uses but three chords, which makes it quite easy to remember. Its simplicity here is frowned upon by some, but it is part of what makes the music magical in my opinion.

The three main chords used in the blues are commonly referred to as being the ONE – FOUR – FIVE chords. This is more simply and commonly written as the Roman numerals, I – IV – V.

You might have come across this before, but just in-case you are wondering what on earth I'm talking about, here's a brief explanation.

The 'C' Major Scale

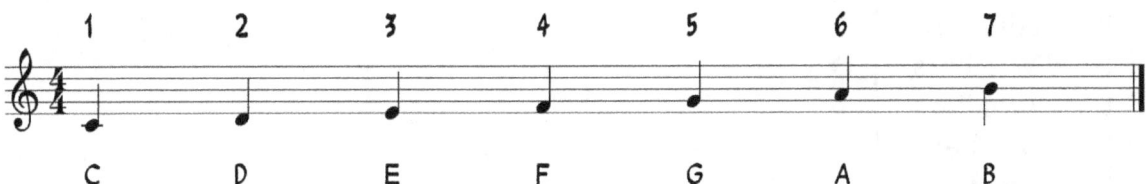

You can see how the 'C' major scale above has had each note numbered, these are the degrees of the scale. When someone uses a Roman numeral as a chord, the number/numeral relates to the note that is numbered accordingly. So in this example the 'I' refers to the 'C' and the 'IV' refers to the 'F'.

I   equals the 'C' chord
II   equals the 'D' chord
III   equals the 'E' chord
IV   equals the 'F' chord
V   equals the 'G' chord
VI   equals the 'A' chord
VII   equals the 'B' chord

The beauty of the system of Roman numerals is that it makes it easy to change the progression into another key. As the designation of 'II' or 'V' is not fixed to any particular chord, it's relative to the key you are playing in.

Here is an example of a basic twelve bar blues progression shown as Roman numerals. Eventually you will get used to thinking about it in these terms, although we will revert to the actual chords to make things easier. You can see below how the three chords fall within the twelve bars, with enough practice this progression will become second nature, just give it time.

A Typical 12-Bar Blues Progression

It consists of...

- 'I' Four bars
- 'IV' Two bars
- 'I' Two bars
- 'V' One bar
- 'IV' One bar
- 'I' Two bars

The use of numerals in place of chords may be new and confusing, but don't worry too much about it, now that we have covered the progression, and you know about the numerals, we will now be referring to the chords used by their actual names. But at least you now hopefully get the idea, which will help you understand things in the future.

For the purpose of this book we will be keeping things in the key of 'C'. With this being a beginners guide, it makes sense for the sake of simplicity. So with that in mind, we will now look at a twelve-bar progression in the key of 'C'.

The I – IV – V chords in the key of 'C' will be C – F – G. Below is the same 12-bar chord progression as before, but this time it is shown with the chords (when in the key of 'C') rather than as numerals.

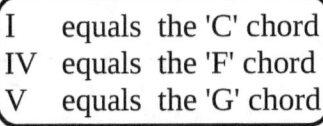

A Typical 12-Bar Blues Progression

Initially at least that's all there is to it, not too hard to remember, although the trick to such styles of playing is that these have to become completely internalized and recalled/used without thought, but that comes with practice.

Although it is only twelve bars long and has but three chords, it still might help you to remember the chord progression by breaking it down into three smaller sections of four bars. Not only because smaller chunks are always easier, but also because the feel of the music does kind of have three separate acts to it within its twelve bars, in a sense at least.

Twelve-Bar Split Into Three Sections

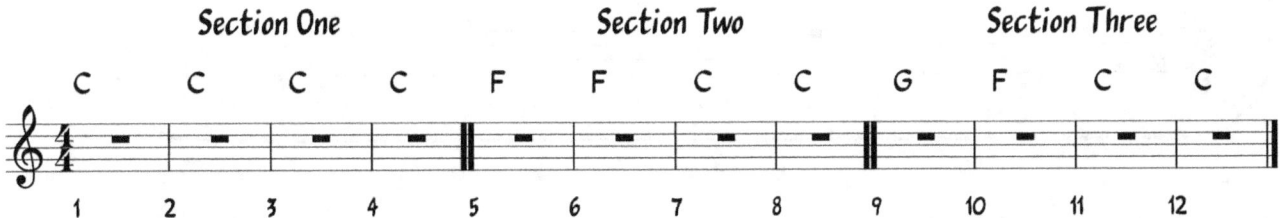

Twelve-Bar Breakdown

1.

The first four bars are all the 'C' chord. In a sense they set the scene, in blues music a little like its asking a question.

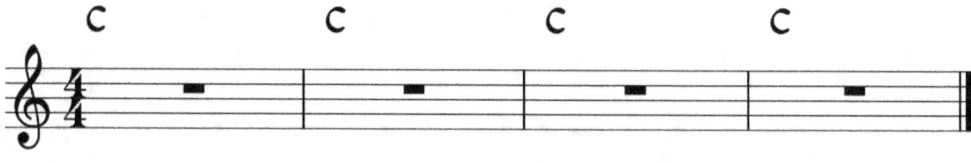

2.

The second four bars are 'F' and 'C' in equal measure. The 'F' is a little like an initial response to the first four bars question and often repeats the same right-hand pattern, although it's often altered to suit the new chord.

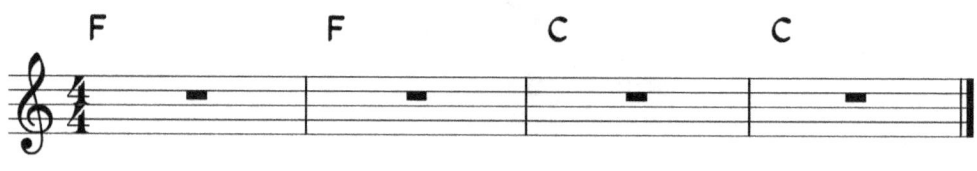

3.

The third four bars are different, the 'G' and the 'F' kind of resolve the question, with the last two bars of 'C' then setting things up for the next twelve bars. The right-hand on these bars is normally different to the pattern you began with to some extent.

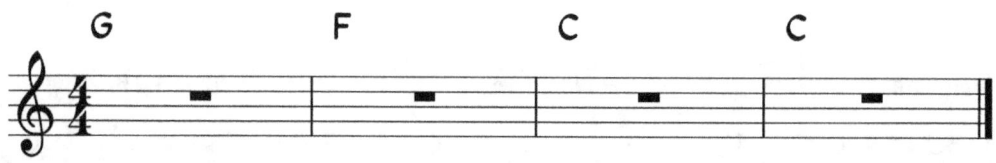

Audio/Fingering

Some examples within the book offer fingering suggestions. These all follow the standard numbering system. Both thumbs are always referred to as being number one, with both the little fingers being number five. So you would count from the inside of your hands outward (with your palms facing down as used on the piano of course).

Finger Numbering

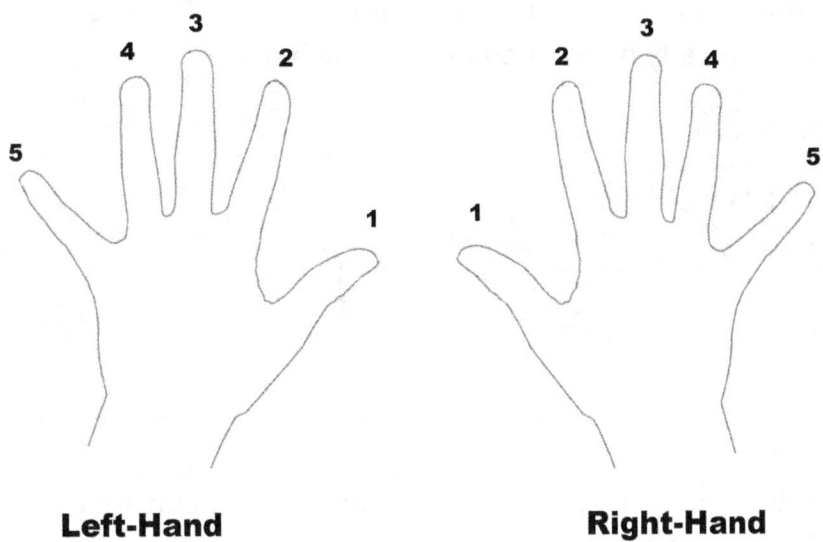

Left-Hand   **Right-Hand**

Audio Examples

The examples that have audio to accompany them, can be identified by having the relevant number next to an audio sign. For access, refer to page 67, for information regarding downloading them from the website.

Example Accompanying Audio Sign

New Orleans Rhythms

New Orleans differs from other forms of blues music, in that it's influenced by strong Caribbean rhythms like the rumba. So although you might find some similar chord progressions and even riffs, the feel of the music is quite unique to itself. There are many rhythm patterns that you will need to learn, the timing is often syncopated, and a little trickier than some music, but we'll look at the timing and how to count, once you get the feel, it becomes second nature.

Timing/Counting

The music here will be using 4/4 timing, so each bar will consist of four beats, which would be naturally be counted out as shown below...

Count for Quarter Notes

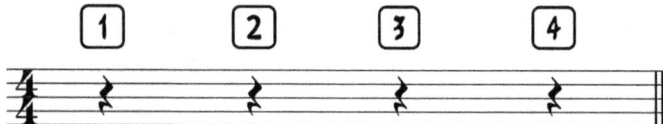

If we then divide each beat by half, we then have eight quavers (or eighth notes) per bar, counted out as shown below...

Count for Eighth Notes

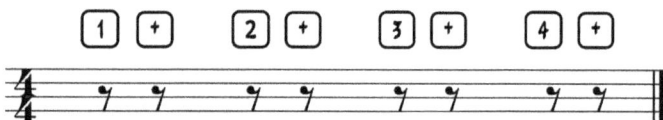

Rumba Style Rhythm

With the counting above in-mind, from here we can look at this common rumba type rhythm. The first two notes are worth 1½ beats each, with the second note starting half-way through beat two. The last note is worth one beat.

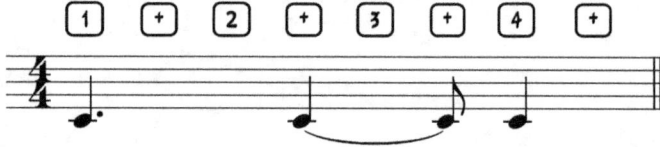

Count for Rumba Rhythm Simplified

Practice the timing of this initially without worrying about what notes are involved, as it's important to get the feel of this down. I suggest using some form of metronome to better hear the beat. Start off slowly, perhaps around 80 bpm and then move up to about 120 bpm.

Count for this is...

First Note: **one and two**
Second Note: **and three and**
Third Note: **four and**

Once you are happy with the timing, practice it while moving through the changes, with a pretty standard twelve-bar blues chord progression. Again, I would suggest a metronome or some form of beat to follow along to, as it will help get the timing right, and keep it tight.

New Orleans Bass Style 1

Now that you have the feel of the timing, it's time to turn it into a proper New-Orleans bass-line for the left-hand. It still consists of three notes, and uses the same timing as practiced, we are just now using a combination of notes to bring it to life. It consists of the root note, the third, and the fifth. These are the notes that make up a basic major chord, except they are just being played in order instead.

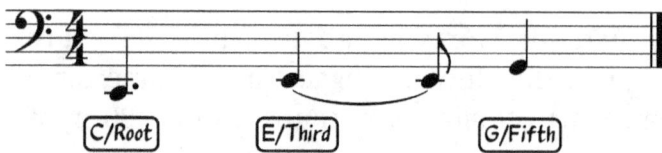

Fingering Suggestions

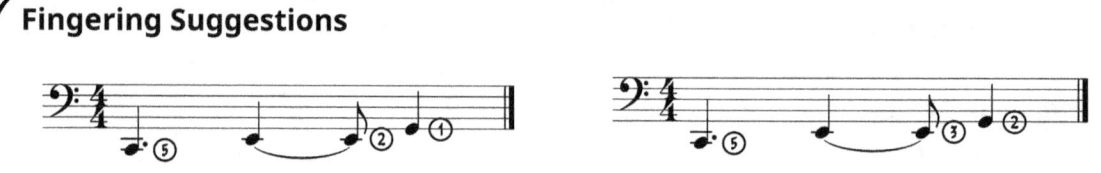

There are two options here. The first version uses 5+2+1 and the second uses 5+3+2. Both of these work fine, so it will be up to your own preference. I feel the first is more comfortable, but the second leaves the thumb free, which can help if you extend the pattern further, although that isn't an issue her

Practice this pattern over a 12-bar chord progression. Start off at whatever speed you feel comfortable, but don't rush it, this kind of thing isn't necessarily played especially fast anyway.

Bass Style 1 - With Chords 1

Time to add the right-hand to the left, starting off with some simple chord patterns. New Orleans music tends to be heavily syncopated, so the interaction between the right and left hands will involve various syncopated rhythms.

Bass Style 1 - With Chords 2

Bass Style 1 - With Chords 3

Bass Style 1 - With Chords 4

Chords

So far we have only used major chords, so let's introduce both the six and seven chords, without which you can't create the right 'blues' sound. You might well know these already, so please feel free to skip past this, but if not, read on.

Sixth chord

A six chord, is a major chord with the addition of the 6th degree of the major scale. The 6th degree of a major scale, is the sixth note along when counting from the root note of the scale and moving up sequentially.

Sixth Degree Shown Within 'C' Major Scale

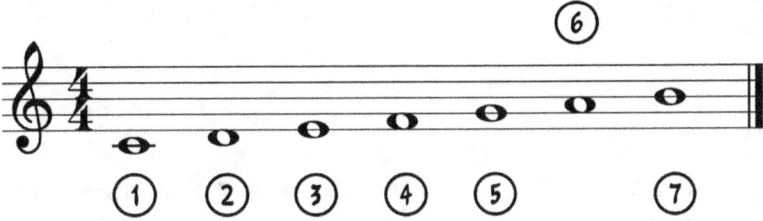

So in order to form a six chord, all you need to do is take a major chord and simply add the 6th. In this case, we are looking at the 'C' scale, and so the chord 'C6'.

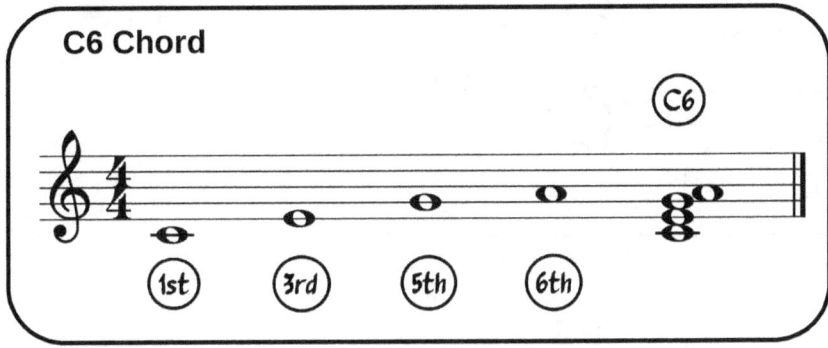

Chord Inversions

Because a six chord consists of four notes, there are therefore four different possible positions/inversions that it can be played in.

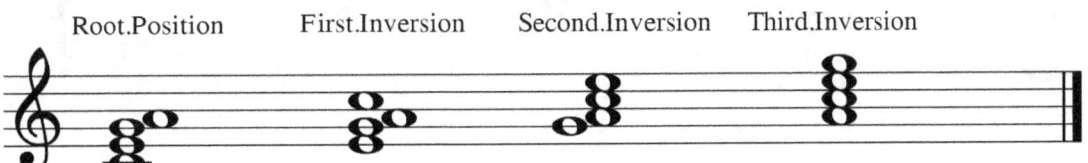

Seventh Chord

The major seventh isn't generally used within blues music – although there are exceptions – so when you hear a seventh chord mentioned, it will refer to the dominant seventh shown below. This note would be found within the Mixolydian mode, but keeping it simple, all you need to know is that it's a flat-seventh. This is seen written just as 'C7'.

Shown Within The Scale

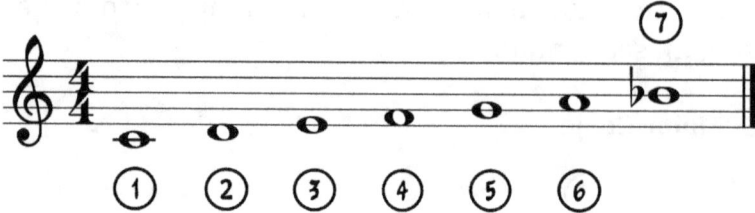

In order to form a seven chord, take a major chord and simply add the flat-seven (also known as the dominant seventh) In this case we are looking at the 'C' scale, and so the chord 'C7'.

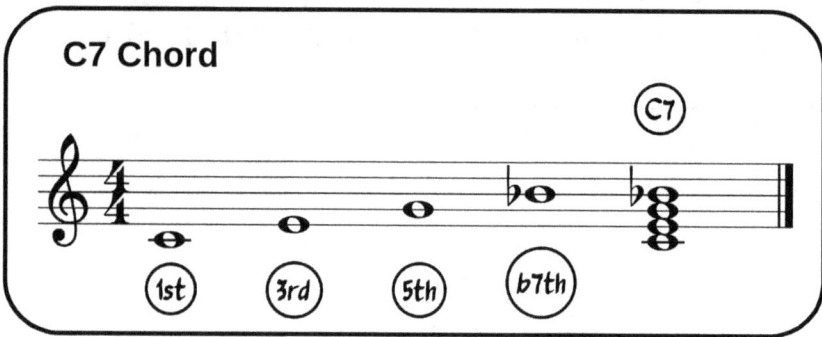

Chord Inversions

Dominant seven chords are created from four notes, therefore it has four possible inversions (positions it can be played in).

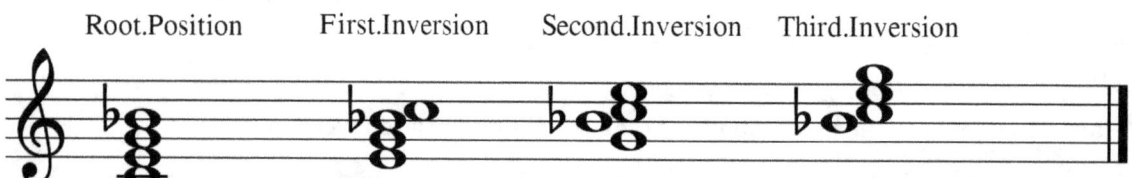

Bass Style 1 - With Chords 5

Here we have a twelve-bar example that uses a combination of rhythms, but now we have both the sixth and seventh chords included.

Blue Rumba

Here we have longer example, that uses a combination of the rhythmic chord patterns, but with major, six and seventh chords.

Blue Rumba continued...

Second 12 Bars

Chord Runs

A common technique you will hear in New Orleans blues is the use of arpeggio type runs going down the chord. These are sometimes referred to as a broken chord, as although all the notes of a chord are used, they aren't played together to create the chord as a whole, but rather played separately instead, in order, normally in quite a fast manner.

This is a simple 'C Maj' chord in a broken pattern. In this example it starts with the root at the top, followed by the other notes of the chord in order, finishing back with the root note an octave lower.

Broken C Chord

Timing/Count

The entire run here takes the space of one beat. As far as the timing is concerned, this is divided into two parts. The first half (eighth note/quaver) is divided into eighth note triplets, with the second half (eighth note/quaver) being the single last note.

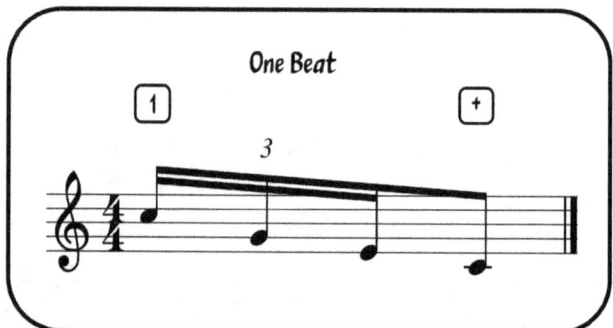
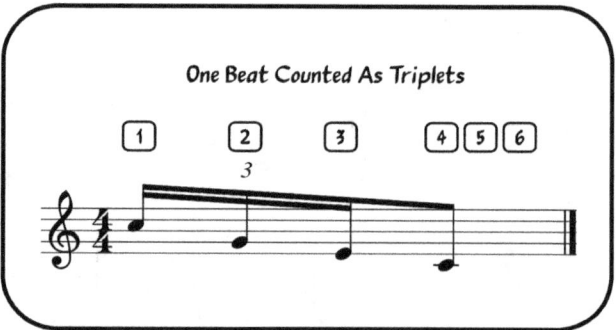

NOTE

This might look a lot harder than it is, so I would suggest listening to this kind of thing first, as it will help to copy it. Learning it that way, rather than concentrating on trying to count out timing should be easier, but we will look at the timing in relation to the left-hand on the next page.

Both Hands Timing

Here the count/timing of both hands have been shown together, so you can see how they interact together.

Timing/Count With Both Hands (Example One)

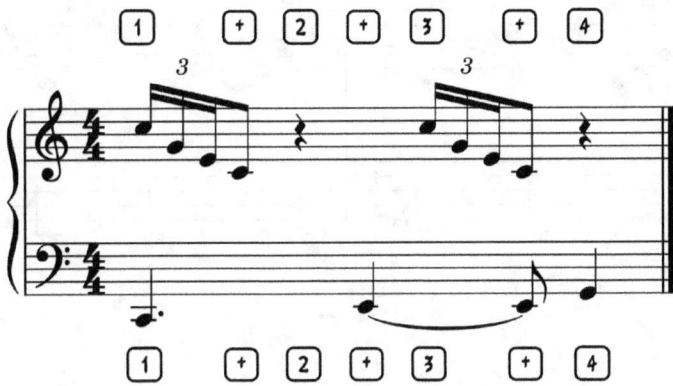

Timing/Count With Both Hands (Example Two)

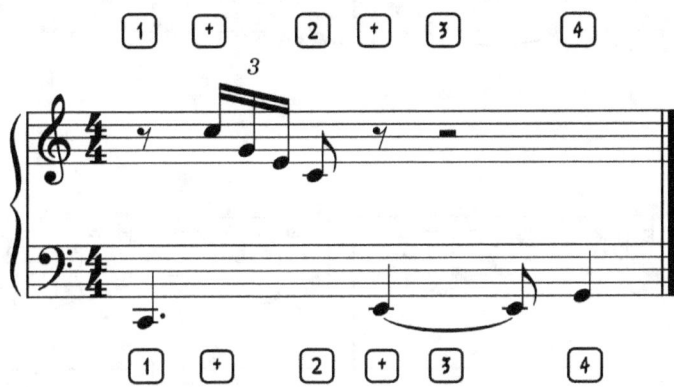

> **Fingering Suggestion**
>
> With the distance covered and the stretch required, there aren't many options with regard to this, so 5+3+2+1 will always work nicely.
>
>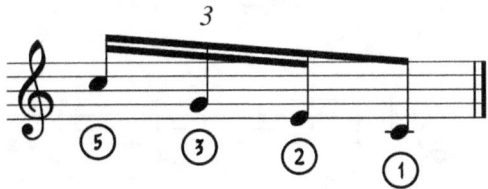

Chord Runs (Example 1)

An exercise to practice some broken chord runs over the left-hand.

Chord Runs (Example 2)

Another exercise to practice some chord runs, this time using the second version shown on the previous pages.

Holding Notes Of The Chord

Sometimes the notes of the chord can be held down as they are played, so you add one note at a time until the chord is complete. As to which you should use (held or broken) is often down to taste, and perhaps the speed of the piece and what is following on immediately after. But there is little technical difference in playing them either way.

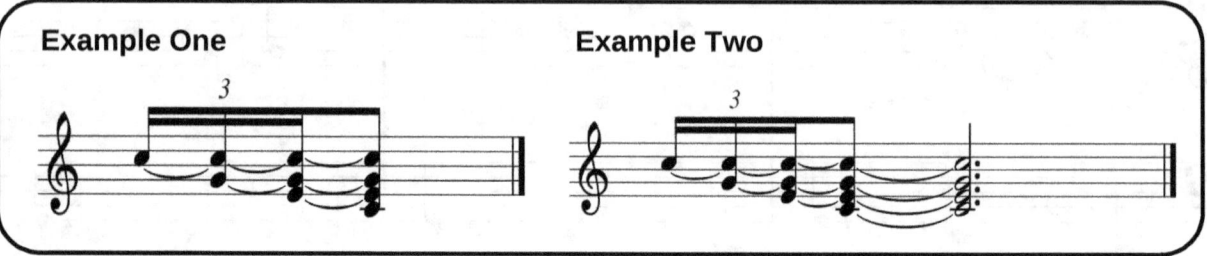

Starting Points

Be aware that despite the examples so far starting with the root note of the cord, you won't necessarily start with the root note all the time.

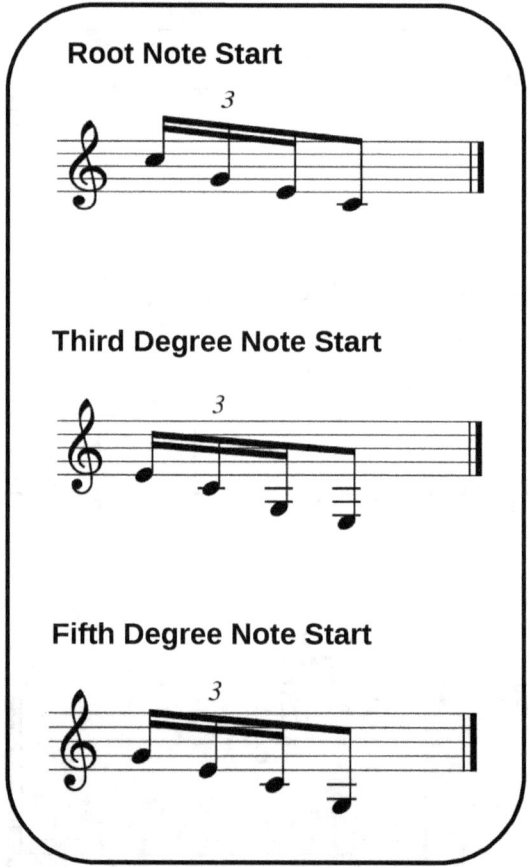

The Broken Blues

The following twelve-bar blues uses the same rumba style left-hand pattern we have looked at so far, with a mixture of chords and runs with the right-hand.

Broken Blues continued...

Second 12 Bars

Broken Run Riffs

Taking the same broken chord type pattern we have used up to now, we can add to it, and create more complex and interesting patterns/riffs. There's a huge amount of possible variations, but here are a few examples to practice, along with suggestions for the fingering. Get them down first, before adding the left-hand on the next pages.

Example One

Example Two

Example Three

Example Four

Example Five

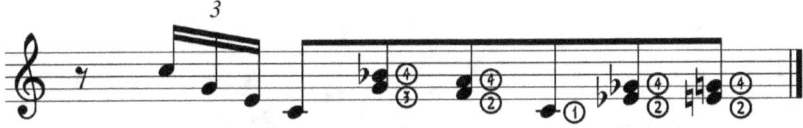

Example Six

Broken Blues 2

This example uses a combination of the riffs we have looked at on the previous page, over the top of the rumba style left-hand.

Broken Blues 2 continued...

Mardi Gras Type Groove

The Mardi Gras is of course an annual festival, whose origins in fact strangely trace back to medieval Europe. In New-Orleans, it is celebrated with very extravagant parades and music, to which a well known song took its title. We will take a look at its feel/groove here.

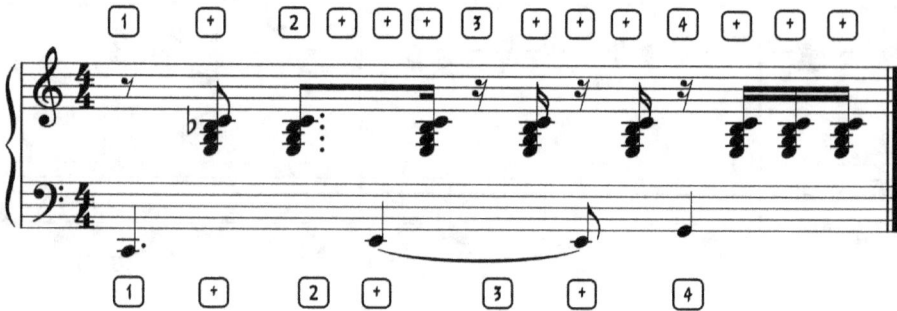

The timing on this isn't the easiest, but once you have it down you're good to go. So I suggest listening to this in order to copy the feel, as playing it from the notation alone will be tricky. It might initially help to split this up into two parts (well maybe, don't quote me on this). Below it's shown in two halves.

First Half

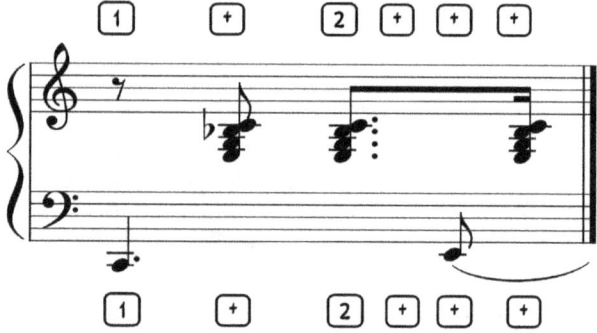

Second Half

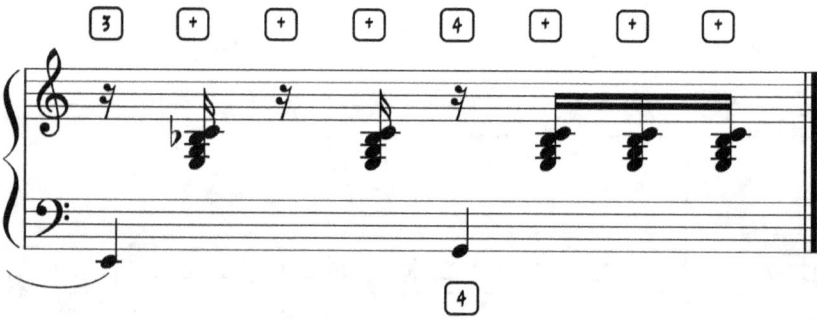

Mardi Gras Type Groove

Try playing the same groove over a 12-bar progression with the chord changes.

Left-Hand Variations

The left-hand bass-line we have been looking at, can of course be varied/changed. Below are some examples of this, without moving too far away from the original. Included are fingering suggestions that might work for you.

1.

2.

3.

4.

Broken/Split Chord Patterns

Rather than playing using just straight chords, a common technique is to play the chords in a split/broken fashion. It's the same chord with the same notes, it's just that they are played separate to each other in a rhythmic fashion.

Variations With Left-hand

1.

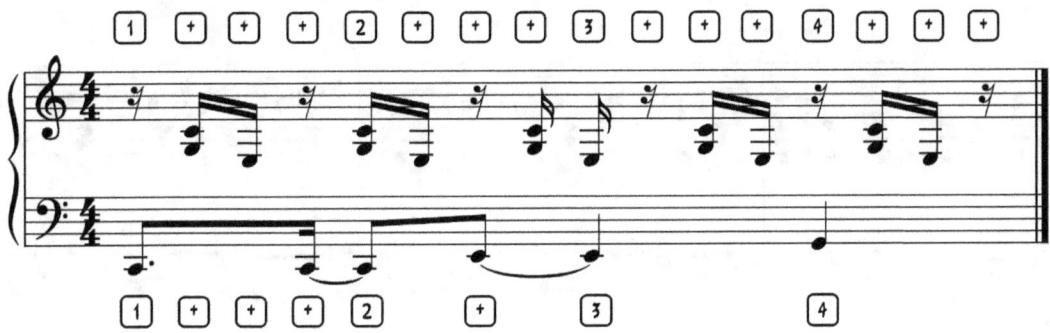

33

Mardi Blues

Mardi Blues continued...

Second 12 Bars

Set-Ups

A set-up in New Orleans music refers to the way that a chord change can have a build up to it, making it sound obvious that something is about to happen. This is normally done when moving from the 'I' chord to the 'IV' chord.

Below are examples of such a thing (there are many). Each of the three shown is essentially the same set-up, starting easier, and then adding more repeated notes with each example. These are really meant to be played as octaves, but to begin with, try it with single notes.

1.

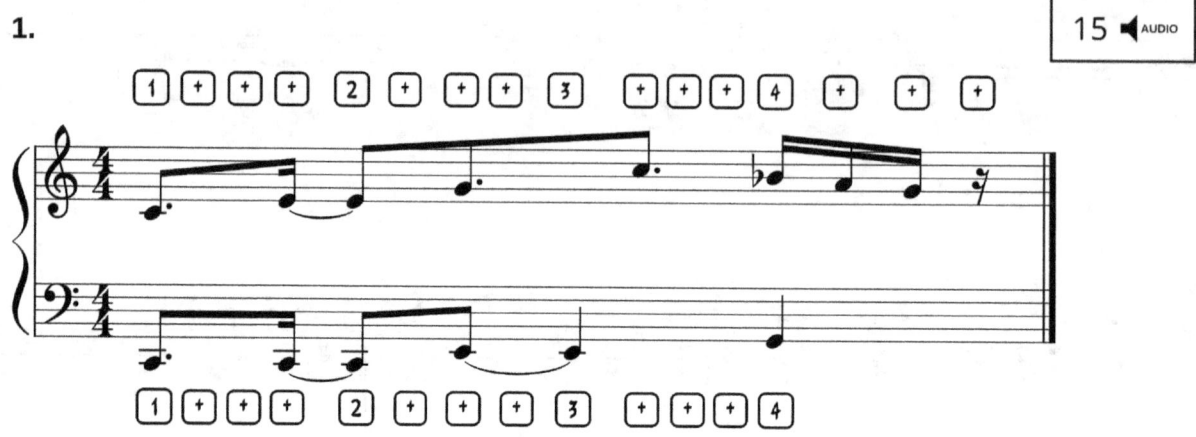

2.

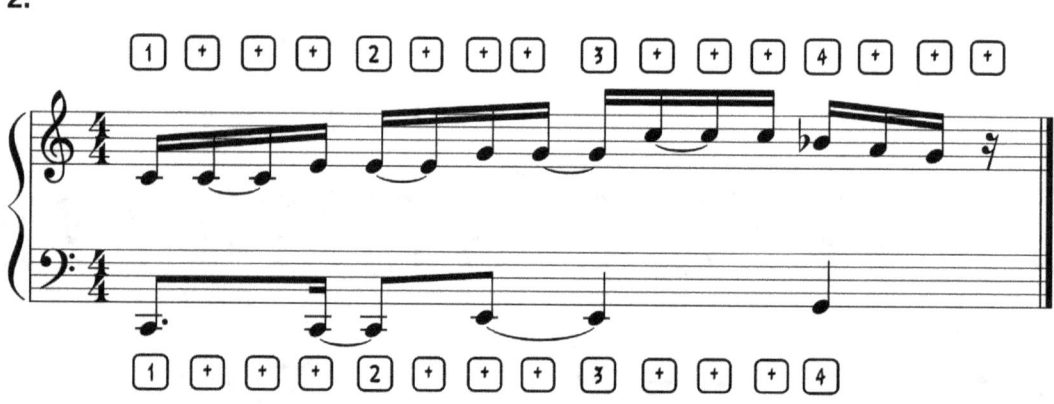

3.

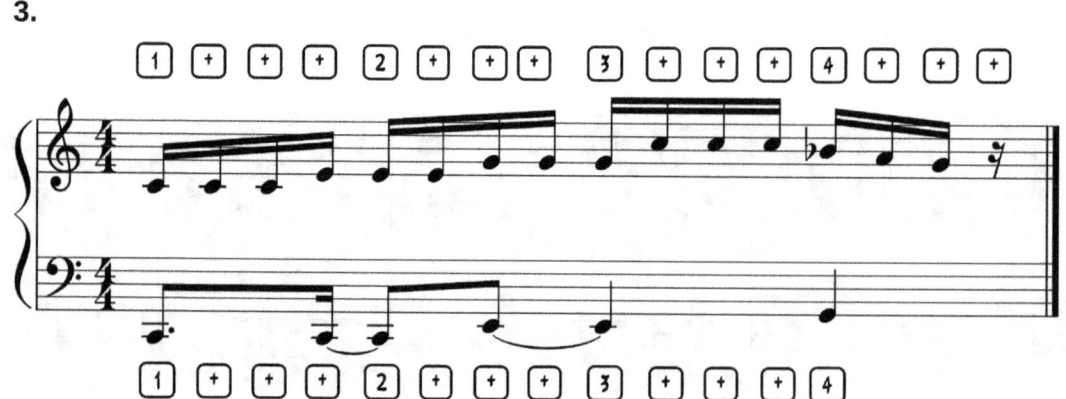

Here we have an example of such a set-up, now within a short example piece (the first six bars of a twelve-bar blues). Notice how it's on the fourth bar leading up to the chord change to the 'F', which is the 'I' to 'IV' chord change.

Below we have an example that uses octaves instead of the single notes. It has a much larger and harder hitting sound, and is how it would generally be done. It's up to you if you want to try and play them as such, or keep to single notes for the time being. As with everything, you start off with an easier version and work up to the harder one in your own time. Due to the stretch involved, fingers five and one would be used throughout for both hands.

Set-Up Using Octaves

Set-Ups Variations

There are many ways of playing a set-up in New Orleans. Here are a couple more examples that you might like to try. Although there is plenty of movement, the left-hand follows the right-hand exactly, so the timing and coordination between them is not an issue.

1.

First played with slightly simplified timing.

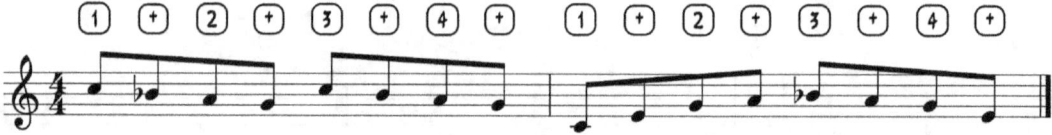

Now with the addition of the left-hand.

2.

This is essentially the same, but the timing has been altered slightly.

Now with the addition of the left-hand.

12-Bar With Set Up

12-Bar With Set Up/Octaves

Triplets

As you may know, a triplet is where each individual beat is divided equally into three. Shown below is a bar of triplets, note how each beat (there are four with the timing being 4/4) is divided equally into three notes.

Example Of Triplets

When considering the timing of these, it might help to think of it as each individual cluster of triplets having the ¾ timing of a waltz. As such, you would count three beats 1 – 2 – 3. But instead of this count of three taking up the entire bar (as in ¾ timing) it is within the space of one beat instead.

Below you can see each of the four beats in the bar sharing the space of each group of triplets. Practice the timing as shown below. Use the count of 1 – 2 – 3 for the right-hand as you play the single bass notes.

Triplet Timing

Triplet Feel Left-Hand

This well known left-hand bass-line has been used on many songs. It can sometimes be found written in 12/8 timing, but for the sake of simplicity we are going to stay with 4/4. Shown below with fingering suggestion.

> **Timing/Count**
>
> You can see below how the triplet sections have their own count of three, within the space of a single beat.
>
>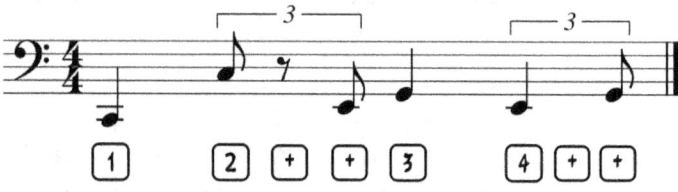

Practice just the left-hand over a twelve-bar progression with the chord changes, until you are comfortable with it.

Triplet Feel Right-Hand

Triplets are often used with the right-hand in fast, repetitive passages. Bear in mind that although it might look very busy/complicated on the page, it's actually far simpler than it first appears.

The examples below shows a set of triplets played over every beat, but essentially all you are doing is repeating the exact same thing three times per beat instead of once. When you think of it that way... it is far easier than the busy notation first makes it appear.

 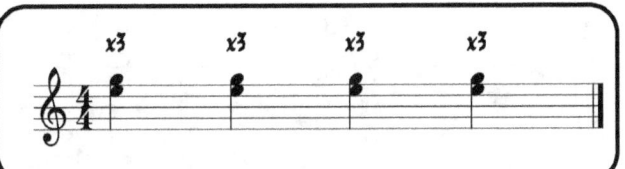

Practice playing repetitive triplets with the right-hand over a twelve-bar progression. Concentrate on getting the timing tight, so use a metronome of some form of drum beat to help.

Triplet Feel Blues

Time to put the left and right-hand together. This is just the left-hand we have looked at, with the simple right-hand from the previous page added over the top. The second page switches from thirds to full chords.

First 12 Bars

Triplet Feel Blues continued...

Second 12 Bars

45

Variations

As with everything, there are a great many variations of this left-hand pattern. Below are some examples of how it might be changed, often within a piece of music itself, as altering the patterns slightly makes the music more interesting.

21 ◀ AUDIO

1.

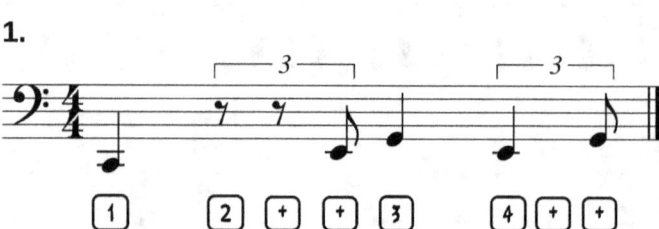

2.

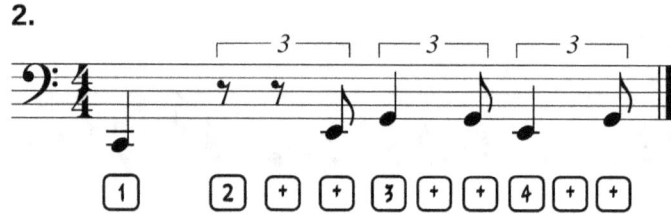

3.

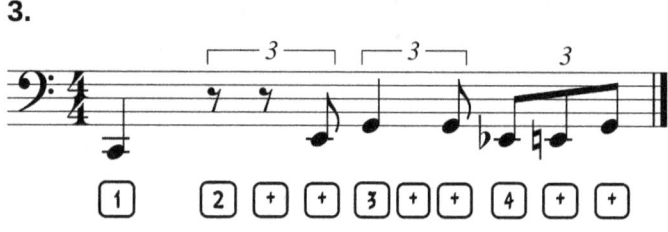

4.

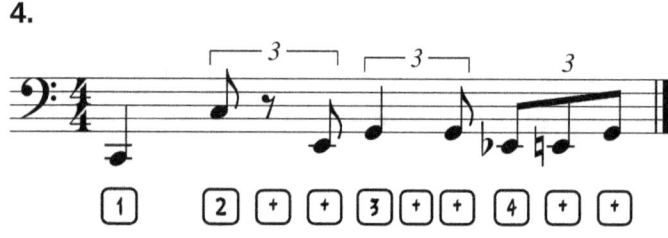

5.

8-Bar Blues

The twelve-bar blues format we have been using so far, might be the most common blues progression (some blues is often referred to as twelve-bar blues after all) but it isn't the only format, as we also have the eight-bar blues.

There are probably more variations of an eight-bar progression than the twelve-bar (perhaps), but here are two of the more common ones you might encounter.

Version One As Numerals

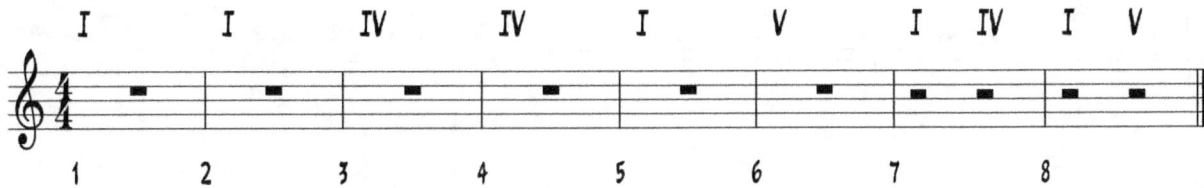

Version One As Chords

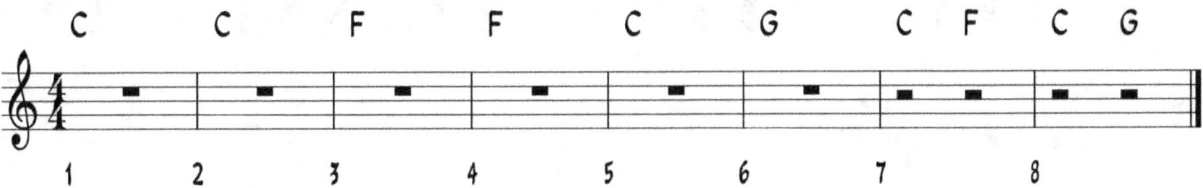

Version Two As Numerals

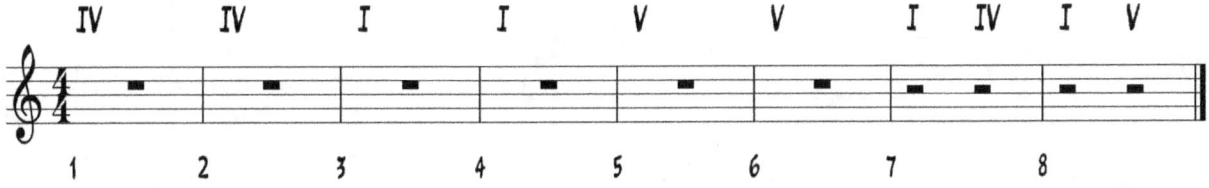

Version Two As Chords

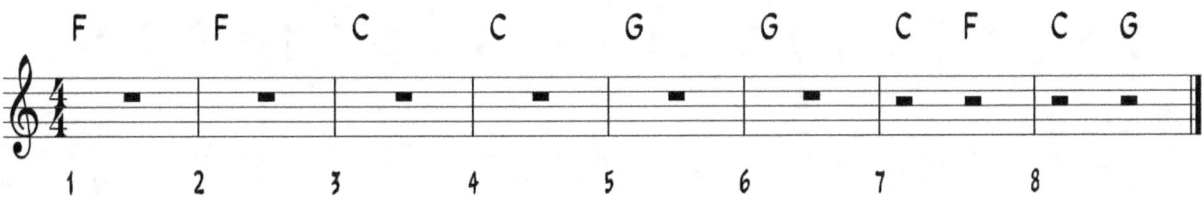

8-Bar Blues One

Here we are using the same left-hand and right-hand patterns as the previous example piece, but now it's played over an eight-bar progression instead.

8-Bar Blues Two

This has similar patterns (with some variations) but it's using the second version of the chord progression. This is more unusual, as it begins on the 'IV' chord.

8-Bar Blues 2 continued...

Second 8 Bars

Second-Line Groove

The term 'Second-Line' refers to the tradition of parades found in New Orleans, so called because it came after the first-line. Such a parade will feature a brass band along with drummers who play off the marching beat that can then inspire the band itself. Such drumming styles and rhythms found their way into New Orleans rhythm and blues music during the 50s. Here we will look at a 'second-line' groove that can be found in New Orleans piano.

Below you have the basic marching beat, with the left-hand alternating with the right-hand. The left-hand bass-line switches between the root note and the fifth below it, while the right-hand plays a chord.

Basic Pattern

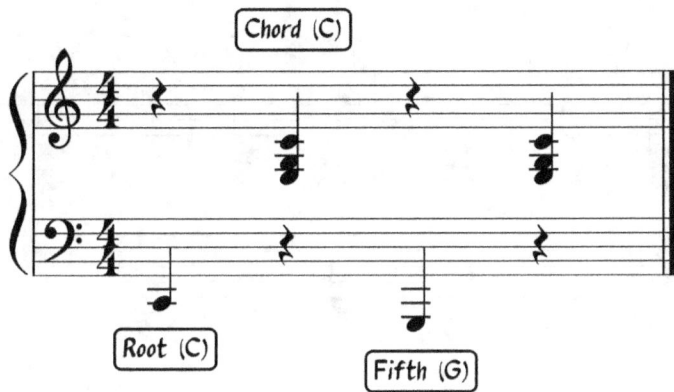

At this point it's all very simple, just a basic beat with each note/chord directly on each beat. Have a quick play through this over a twelve-bar progression on the next page, just to get it lodged into your head before we go and add a little to it. Notice though that the chord progression is slightly different, with the 'V' chord for both bars nine and ten.

Chord Progression Variation

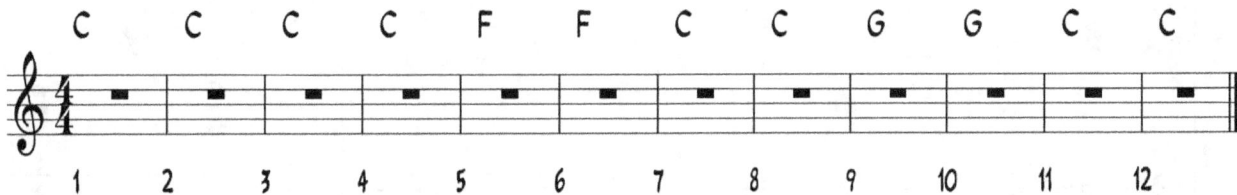

Basic Second-Line Groove

Second-Line Groove Left-Hand

It's time to add a little something to this, try the following patterns for size. The first two start off the same in the first bar, but with different things happening in the second. The third changes the whole timing somewhat. I'd suggest getting used to the idea of this using single notes first, before trying it in octaves (naturally using 5+1 fingers) and then introduce the right-hand afterwards when ready.

Version One (Single Notes)

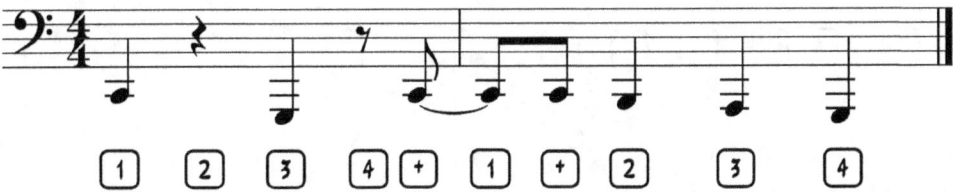

Version One (Octaves)

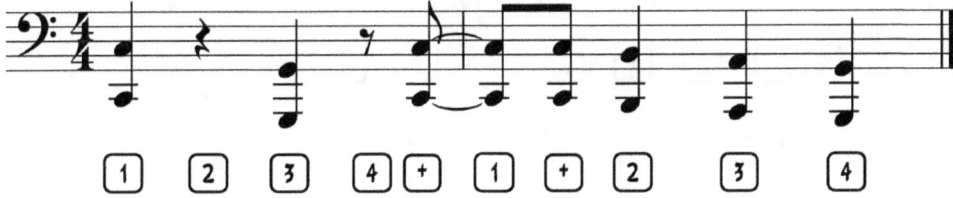

Version One (Combined With The Right-Hand)

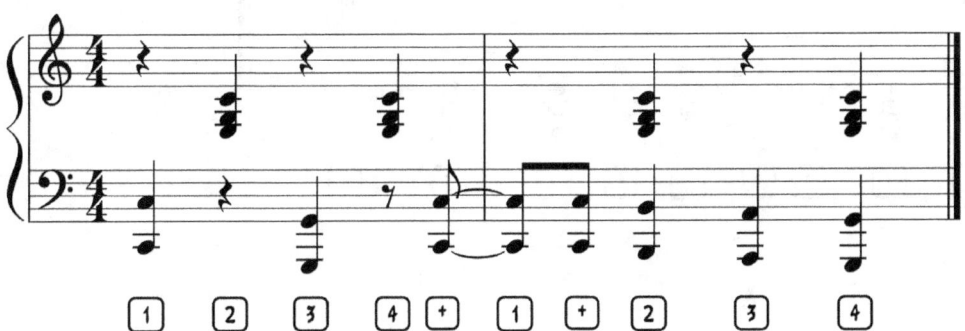

Version Two

This is a variation of the first pattern, but this time the bass-line walks upwards in the second bar, instead of downwards as in the first version.

Version Two (Single Notes)

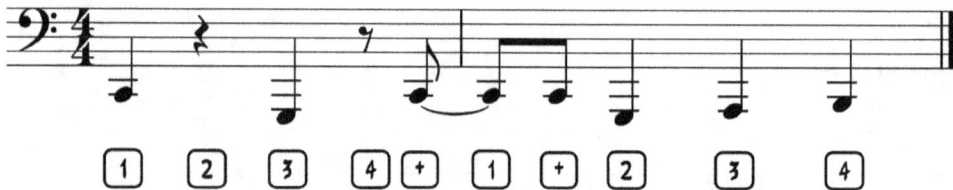

Version Two (Octaves)

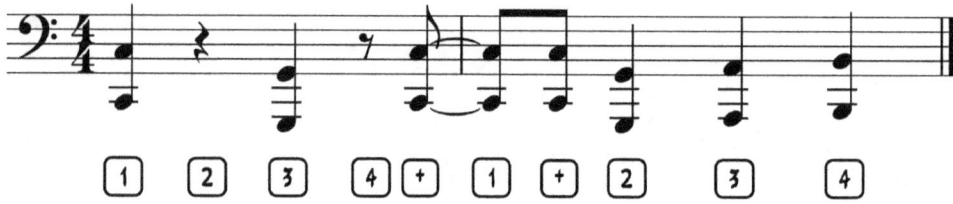

Version Two (Combined With The Right-Hand)

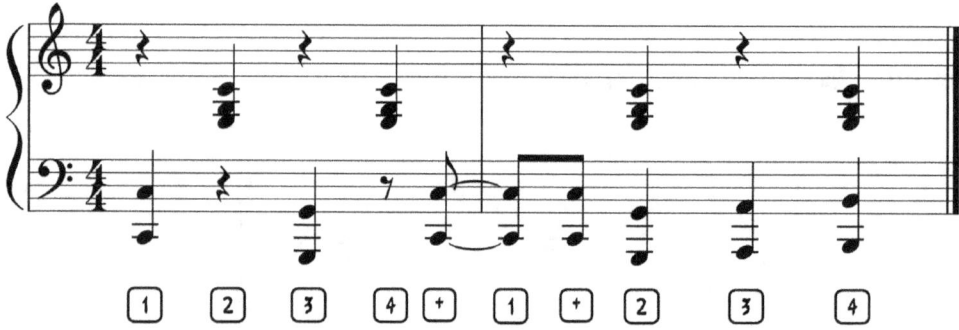

Version Three

This is a variation on the first pattern, but this pattern uses a slightly different rhythm to the previous two, which works well when mixed in-between to create interest.

Version Three (Single Notes)

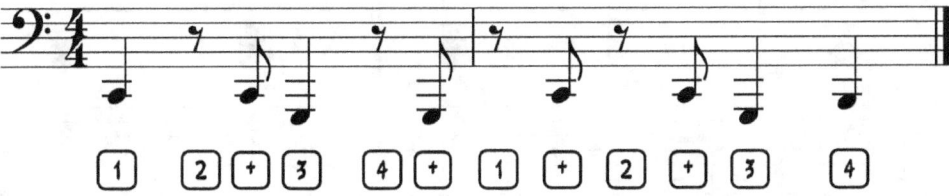

Version Three (Octaves)

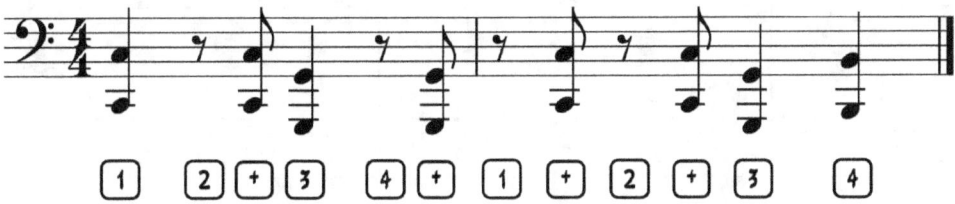

Version Three (Combined With The Right-Hand)

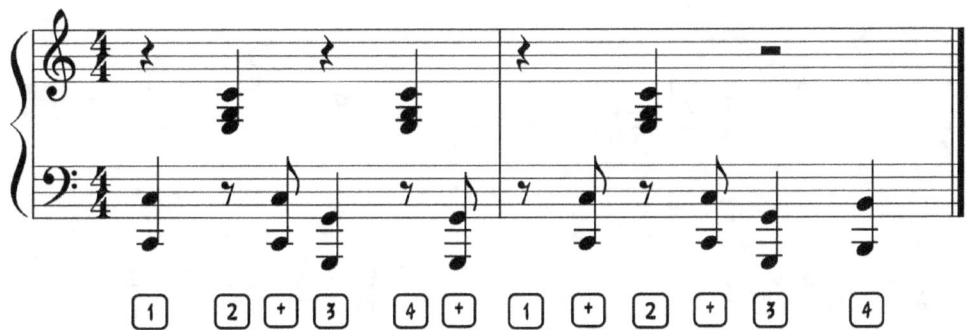

Second-Line Song

First 12 Bars

Second-Line Song continued...

Second 12 Bars

Second-Line Song continued...

Third 12 Bars

New Orleans Groove

Here we have another left-hand pattern. Starting from the root note, it moves in a descending pattern down to the root note an octave lower. Most of the action is in the first bar, with only a single note at the start of the second. There is a reason for this though, as it makes room for the right-hand to come into play, but we will look at that afterwards. Again, this is meant to be played in octaves, but to ease into it, get the idea with single notes first.

Groove Pattern (With Count/Fingering)

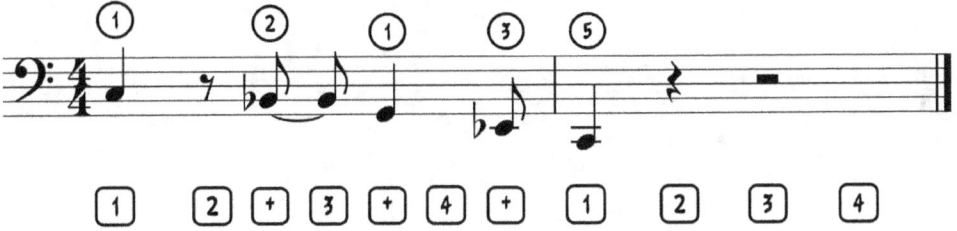

Try practicing this pattern (just the left-hand) over a twelve-bar progression, before moving on and adding anything with the right-hand. Notice that the progression keeps the 'V' chord for both bars nine and ten.

12-Bar Song 1

Here you have the same left-hand, but now introducing the right-hand. You can see how it fits in when the left-hand takes a break.

12-Bar Song 2

This example is similar, but with the right-hand increasing in difficultly.

Variations/Additions

Example One

To take this a little further you could add a little bit, with a variation of the left-hand that moves back upwards, rather than downwards.

Example Two

You can also add an extra note to lead into the pattern. Shown below in the second bar, the seventh is played at the end of the bar, just before the pattern starts again in the third bar.

Example Three

Shown here with a chord change to the 'IV'. Using the seventh of the new chord in the previous bar before the actual chord change.

> Try these changes with the example piece on the next pages. Notice that it has been notated with the left-hand in octaves, these are optional, but recommended.

The Professor Blues

The Professor Blues continued...

Second 12 Bars

Practice Suggestions

Practice Time

I will state the obvious and say that to progress and improve at anything you need to spend time doing that thing. So needless to say that the more time you spend on the piano the better you will get. But I will say one thing, consistency is the key. The best way to progress is to practice every day, this keeps everything fresh in your mind and will really help push you forward. And when I say every day, it doesn't necessarily mean hours and hours (although if you can, great, the more, the merrier) just put in whatever you can spare, even ten minutes if that's all you have, the main thing is to keep it regular without large gaps in-between.

Metronome

Using a metronome while practicing is highly recommended. The use of one will really help with keeping the timing tight throughout and also when learning a part that has timing you are unaccustomed to. When I say metronome, use whatever you have, which may literally be a mechanical metronome or one on an electric instrument or even an app on your phone. Playing along to a drum backing is also an option, and there are a few drum tracks available to download, although these are of course at set tempos.

Listen To The Music

To really get the feel of any style of music, it is vital that you listen to it as much as possible. This really helps you internalize the sound, which in turn will help enable you to recreate it on the piano. There really is no substitute for this, no amount of sheet music can portray the feel of a piece of music as well as simply listening to it can.

Suggested Listening

Without doubt one of the most important things you can do when learning a style of music is to listen to it, and I mean a lot. This may sound obvious, but you really want to make a point of listening to the music that you are trying to play. While you can learn songs merely from reading sheet music, the dots and dashes really don't convey the feeling of the music the same way. The brain absorbs the sounds that you hear, which makes it far easier to then translate that sound onto the piano.

Below are a few suggestions of what to listen to, including the biggest well known names in regard to New Orleans piano, these would certainly be my starting point. Listening to most albums from these pianists will help you further your game (although I would suggest the more piano based ones). Some sheet music for the likes of Professor Longhair, Dr. John and James Booker are available if you look for them, as either published books or note for note transcriptions available from the internet.

Artists

Professor Longhair : 1918 – 1980

Dr John: 1941 - 2019

Fats Domino: 1928 - 2017

James Booker: 1939 - 1983

Jon Cleary: 1967 – Present

Dom Pipkin: Present

Henry Butler: 1948 - 2018

Allen Toussaint: 1938 - 2015

Downloadable Audio

Audio files based on the examples within the book are available to download from the website in MP3 format, simply follow the instructions below.

To access and download the MP3 audio files, simply visit the website...

www.tylermusic.co.uk

- Click on audio downloads
- Select the relevant book title
- Enter the password... **neworleans862**
- Click on the download icon

Once downloaded please save them for future use.

Downloadable Audio Files

1) Rumba Timing
2) Bass Style1
3) Bass Style.1 Chords.1
4) Bass Style.1 Chords.2
5) Bass Style.1 Chords.3
6) Bass Style.1 Chords.4
7) Bass Style.1 Chords.5
8) Blue Rumba
9) Chord Run Ex.1
10) Chord Run Ex.2
11) Broken Blues
12) Broken Blues 2
13) Mardi Gras Groove
14) Mardi Blues
15) Set-Up 1
16) Set-Up 2
17) 12-Bar Set-Up
18) 12-Bar Set-Up/Octaves
19) Bass 12-Bars
20) Triplet Feel Blues
21) Bass Variations
22) 8-Bar Blues
23) 8-Bar Blues 2
24) Second-Line Basic
25) Second Line L/H 1
26) Second Line L/H 2
27) Second Line L/H 3
28) Second Line Song
29) New Orleans Groove
30) 12-Bar Song 1
31) 12-Bar Song 2
32) Professor Blues

Want to learn more blues piano...

The complete blues piano is a comprehensive guide to playing and improvising blues piano. It covers the fundamental principles of the blues and includes in-depth theory and techniques, along with example blues pieces to learn/study with downloadable audio. Ranging from fast boogie-type blues to slow blues, Chicago through to New Orleans, beginners to intermediate, this has it covered. 240 pages.

Start playing authentic blues today

Tyler music.co.uk

For further piano books (including spiral bound editions)
sheet music and information on blues
and boogie woogie music
visit the website at…

www.tylermusic.co.uk

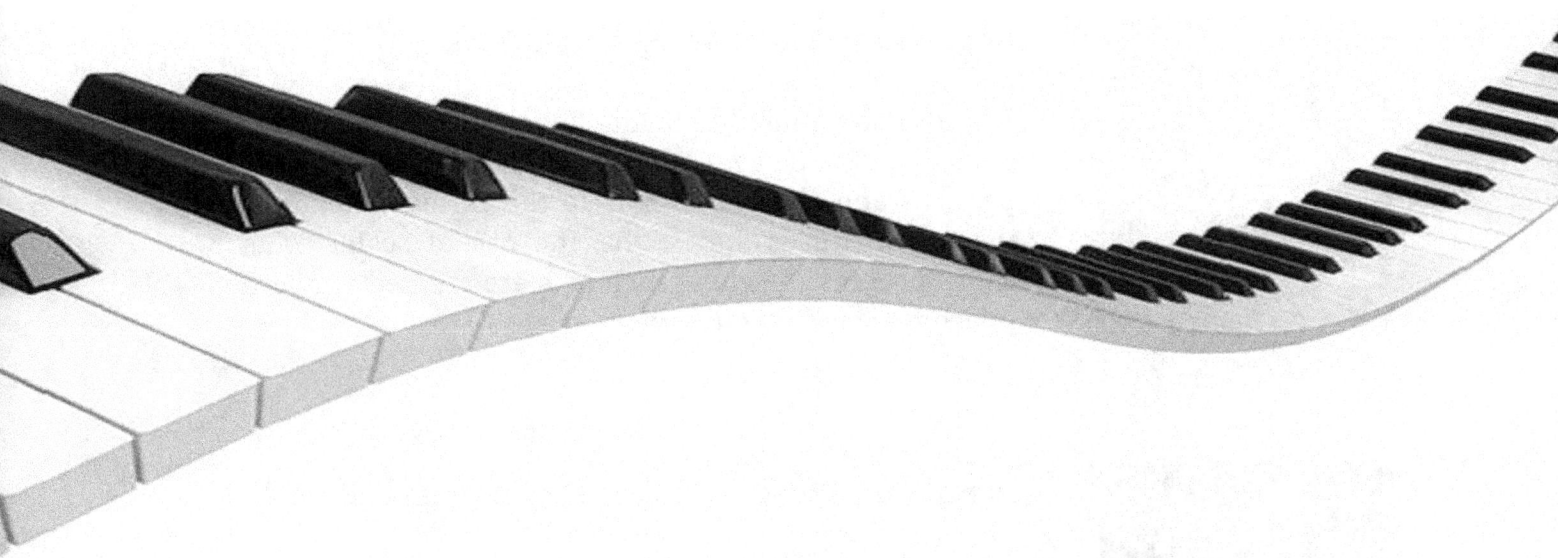

**Follow us on Facebook for updates
and information on latest releases.**

Also Available

Improvising Boogie-Woogie Vol. One

Learn to play boogie-woogie like the best of them. If you want to play boogie like Albert Ammons, Axel Zwingenberger or Jools Holland then this is the series for you. The first volume in a series of books to teach boogie-woogie piano, from the basics to more advanced techniques and everything in-between, this will give you the help and material you need.

Improvising Boogie-Woogie Vol. Two

The ultimate guide to playing boogie-woogie continues with volume-two, adding more left-hand patterns and right-hand riffs, including aspects like the walking-bass pattern, a little stride, rolling chords, using tenths and more complex rhythmic ideas.

Improvising Boogie-Woogie Vol. Three

The ultimate guide to playing boogie-woogie continues with volume-three, adding even more left-hand patterns and right-hand riffs to the series. Looking at the use of thirds and sixths, the use of scaler other chord progressions how such riffs are created and how to begin to create your own.

Improvising Boogie-Woogie: The Complete Edition

All three volumes in one edition. Available as perfect bound and spiral bound (spiral available through the website only). Learn to play boogie-woogie like the best of them. If you want to play boogie like Albert Ammons, Axel Zwingenberger or Jools Holland then this is the series for you. From the basics to more advanced techniques and everything in-between.

Easy Boogie-Woogie   For Beginners

Easy boogie-woogie takes the beginning boogie pianist through their first steps into the timeless style. It covers the basics with easy to understand clear explanations and includes example pieces throughout that start off easy and gradually increase in difficulty while adding extra elements. With downloadable audio,why not start learning boogie-woogie today.

Easy Blues Piano   For Beginners

Learn to play the blues with this beginners guide for the piano. It covers the very basics of the blues, introducing the various elements that create the twelve-bar blues sound. It starts off easy, so even a relative beginner can dive in, and gradually introduces new ideas. With downloadable audio,why not start learning blues today.

Easy Rock 'N' Roll   For Beginners

Easy rock 'n' roll is for the beginner taking their first steps into the timeless sound of rock 'n' roll piano. Covering the basics with easy to understand clear explanations on how to play in the style of the likes of Jerry Lee Lewis and Little Richard. It includes example pieces throughout that start off easy and gradually increase in difficulty, while adding extra elements along the way. With downloadable audio

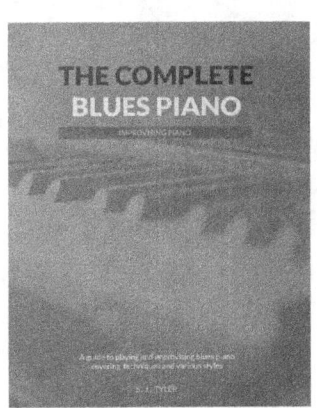

The Complete Blues Piano

The complete blues piano is a comprehensive guide to pl11 ptaying and improvising blues piano. It covers the fundamental principles of the blues and includes in-depth theory and techniques, along with example blues pieces to learn/study with downloadable audio. Ranging from fast boogie-type blues to slow blues, Chicago through to New Orleans, beginners to intermediate, this has it covered.

Piano Blues Scales

The ultimate guide to learning the blues scales for the piano. The scales are clearly shown and explained in all keys for both major and minor scales along with fingering suggestions. But it doesn't stop there, here we go further and include ideas like the combined scales and methods of how to practice and use the scales in a more musical and practical real world fashion.

Bite Sized Specifics – Blues Piano/Walking-Bass

Learn to play the walking-bass for blues piano with the first in a series that concentrates on specific aspects of blues piano. Concentrating on the left-hand, it looks at what the walking-bass is, how it is created and various ways to which you can employ it in a blues environment.

Bite Sized Specifics – Blues Piano/Stride-Piano

Learn to play blues piano using the left-hand stride style. The second in a series that concentrates on a specific aspect of blues piano. Concentrating on the left-hand, it looks at what stride is and how it is created and various ways to which you can employ it in a blues environment.

Bite Sized Specifics – Blues Piano/Right-Hand Vol.1

Learn to play blues piano with the third in a series that concentrates on specific aspects of blues piano. Concentrating on the right-hand, it concentrates on the important aspect of comping, which is the more rhythmic side of blues with an emphasis on the important use of chords and repetitive patterns/riffs that form the backbone of the music.

Tyler Music – Blues & Boogie-Woogie Piano

www.ingramcontent.com/pod-product-compliance
Lightning Source LLC
Chambersburg PA
CBHW081406070526
44583CB00020B/2696